Neoteny: Poems

poems by

Emily K. Michael

Finishing Line Press
Georgetown, Kentucky

Neoteny: Poems

*For Michele,
a friend in difficult times*

Copyright © 2019 by Emily K. Michael
ISBN 978-1-64662-083-8 First Edition
All rights reserved under International and Pan-American Copyright Conventions. No part of this book may be reproduced in any manner whatsoever without written permission from the publisher, except in the case of brief quotations embodied in critical articles and reviews.

ACKNOWLEDGMENTS

"4PM," *Saw Palm: Florida Arts & Literature*
"Ajeen," "Anniversary in St. Augustine," "Faith," and "Small Hours," *Nine Mile Magazine*
"Cello," *Artemis Journal*
"Green time," *Bridge Eight*
"I Begin to Understand Jo March," finalist for the 2018 Atlantis Award, *The Poet's Billow*
"Inside Jokes," *The Fem*
"Kiwano," *The Hopper*
"Mint" and "Natural Compliance," *South Carolina Review*
"A Phenomenology of Blindness," *Rogue Agent*
"Trading Threes," *The Deaf Poets Society*

Publisher: Leah Maines
Editor: Christen Kincaid
Cover Art: Chelsea Whiteman, Chelsea Whiteman Photography
Author Photo: Chelsea Whiteman, Chelsea Whiteman Photography
Cover Design: Elizabeth Maines McCleavy

Printed in the USA on acid-free paper.
Order online: www.finishinglinepress.com
      also available on amazon.com

              Author inquiries and mail orders:
                    Finishing Line Press
                        P. O. Box 1626
                Georgetown, Kentucky 40324
                            U. S. A.

Table of Contents

I Begin to Understand Jo March 1
Mint 2
Anniversary in St. Augustine 3
Fig tree 4
I Say Yes 5
Ajeen 6
Citti's Blush 7
Citti's Piano 8
Artifact 9
Practice 10
In This One 11
Gallery 12
Encore 13
Grooming 14
Wood Thrush 15
Faith 16
Inside Jokes 17
Glass of Milk 18
Natural Compliance 19
Trading Threes 20
Sap 21
Antiphon for Emily 22
Small Hours 23
From the Plinth 24
Song 25
Deficiencies 26
When He Calls Me Your Wife 27
Kiwano 28
Blindness Locked Me Out 29
4PM 30
In the Half-Light of Rehearsals 31
Green time 32
A Phenomenology of Blindness 33
Cello 34

I Begin to Understand Jo March

I wanted her wildness—
tramp of russet boots, hair bundled
she defied all ornaments.
        I wanted energy to overturn expectations.

Now all my sisters are mothers
and plump little palms tap at my door,
make auntie nonsense of my name.
        I miss the sisterhood gone.

I ache in that self conscious corner
of my heart, where other joys crowd—
Hope, reckless and springy underfoot,
shoulders old beliefs aside. I recognize
the step of a returning friend.

I tune my ears to his laugh at the gate
and lean against him as we cross the green ground.

Mint

My grandmother's dining room table is covered
by rectangular baking sheets, each lined with plaid
kitchen towels. Bunches of mint still damp from
washing afford the house their fragrance.
I open the screen door and stand in the narrow
hall, shuffling my feet to smooth the upturned
carpet. One hand still gripping the ancient latch
I hail the commonplace: dewy and sharp.

Anniversary in St. Augustine

We blessed the Florida autumn,
ate bacon sandwiches under gray clouds.
I drank hot chai for a sore throat. He held my hand.

We drove two hours to walk the old quarter—
traded thirty dollars for three hundred years.
Hollow houses, tiny plaques, costumed guides interrupted,
joyful crunches on studied gravel.

He wanted to climb the old watchtower,
gamboled up the steps like a boy. I stayed
on the second landing, dizzy with kisses,

In the colonial newspaper office he guided
my hands to a huge wooden printing press.
"I bet we aren't supposed to touch this."
He helped me learn its levers and knobs.

Fig tree

Plump purple teardrops fuzzy in my fingers
Squishy spheres mapped in tactile veins
Momma showed me how to twist them free.

Tiny hard globes cold and green
Momma says we can't pick these.

Branches crooked and waving on the night
Silent companion cupping stars
I've stopped waiting for you to speak.

I Say Yes

Fingers slightly too large to slide
Between mine, the hungry press across the
Console when the car stops—longing limbs immortalize
Separate forms in one eager memory.
Yes to the hand that stirs my decaffeinated chai, the arm that
Extends my winter coat. Yes to lips of forthright question
as we fasten glossy oversized buttons, to unwrung
Dishcloths still smelling of generic Palmolive—a viscous
Green Apple that mingles with the warm water covering
Our white arms. Yes to a play-battle for the ugliest pillow—who
Will heave it across the room to accommodate our books?
To the susurrous of hallway promises and flipping pages, yes.

Ajeen

The *ajeen* shop is the only restaurant open on a flooded street.
And we—its only customers—share a wooden bench, knees
tucked close under the round table. Our *ajeen* stuffed with
chicken, onions, sumac, drips fragrant oil as we raise separate
halves. Your hand quick with the napkin catches the drops
falling on my lap. Your arm crescents my waist, my
body tailored to the curve. My cheek on your plaid shoulder,
you scrape together French phrases from a far-gone course.
Between formal and informal greetings your hand lifts
my chin, brushes my cheek. Lips forget the French and *ajeen*.

Citti's Blush

We caught Citti, gray and kind, peering around a kitchen door
seventy years away. She described first time she saw her husband,

a man already promised in marriage who refused the girl
his parents had chosen—she blushed all over again—
Spoke with brave sweetness: *My heart leapt to see him.*

It was the greeting she adapted for my mother, the refrain we chanted
over her waterstained notebook of vague recipes.
My heart leaps to see you.

Crammed elbow-to-elbow in the dining room we retold the story
of Citti's blush, passing the silver breadbasket of buttered pita,
toasted triangles spongy in our fingers.

Citti's Piano

Braided honey wood holds the Level 1 sheet music,
and watches the man and his niece hurry to the bench
hungry for beloved keys—an old song she doesn't know
the words to. He lets her improvise, happy to be
the bass line. It's the only time they are alone.
Other uncles claim the backgammon board
or the old tree with upward swirling branches.
No one else plays ageless at Citti's piano.

Artifact

In a crowded cabinet the purple cup reigns:
glazed color sharp against the plastic tumblers.
Its dark cavity receives herbal tea, ice cream,
hot lima beans studded with shreds of ham.
I have traced the embossed chevrons of its sides
insensible to heat—
I have tracked the knot of glossy purple
as the cup is lifted down, filled,
held out. I have watched big hands
ferry the small vessel into another
room, to a place created for me.

Practice

Can the slim music rack support
these wide sheets, thrice folded

Does the lamp sitting on the dark
piano wink in welcome or glare

Does the short balding teacher laugh
and tap the vacant bench
out of kindness

Will the teacher's patience outlast
enlarging notes

Small hands long accustomed to the cool keys
now tentative below shaking eyes
corner lamp laughing in bright waves

Light spills over a Chopin
nocturne repositioned
on huge paper—still blurry.

In This One

In this one, my head tilts back
at an angle, and your face peeks
around the curve of my cheek. Your
cheeks curve too, and you're grinning
like a little boy as we take selfies
in the concert hall, proud
of our coordinating finery. Your rich purple shirt
and my soft black scarf, our heavy coats
ready for the night wind, the frantic
teeth-shaking trek to the parking garage.
But that's still to come, after Mozart
and Beethoven and Sibelius. After my fingers
tightly curled around your large hand, my cheek
resting against the fabric of your shirt.
Your curly head tickles my face while we
find comfort in the play of documentation.

Gallery

Two figures occupy the carpet's edge hands locked
behind backs, eyes forward.
White cane cold in my fingers I wait
one-and-a-half steps away.

You see the concentration of color, one asks
lifting his fedora, resting long fingers on his hip.
The reds, the blues, this canvas is wild.

No, no, says the other, fiddling
with her scarf—a series of crocheted loops—
Look at how the objects are laid out. That
little dog in the foreground, somewhat hidden.

Ah yes, he sighs, adjusts the hat,
smooths the folds of his corduroy coat.
A nodding exchange, they glide to the right,
feet almost soundless on the sleek floor.

Encore

Full of grilled fish and lemon mousse we step
        off the curb into the parking lot. A hard
        humid plateau, silent—but for the voice
of a lone performer. Poised within the obliging
shade a mockingbird holds court.
Wild petitioner and minstrel
        he sends forth a cascade of borrowings:
six different songs—one after another. Robust
        proclamations tuning the hot
        metal of unmoved cars. No residents
dare contest his precedence.

Grooming

The leather leash has metal clips that chime
against the chipped brown rail when I secure
my dog to the steps. The two dog brushes ring
signature pitches on the concrete. Blue
rubber oval bounces, barely makes a sound. Metal
comb thuds once—heavy and cold. I choose
the lowest step, stretch my legs, hold my hand
palm-up. Concrete chill cuts through my thin pants.
Dog sniffs, turns, pushes his warm body
against my lap. He rolls back, nose up, tail
thrumming on my calf. I plant fingers
in the notch between his ribs and hip,
lift the blue brush, make him sit. He watches
the birds, head angled toward the stump of a sick
tree. I count the trills, the strokes, the tufts—
old hair moving painlessly away.

Wood Thrush

Hand raises the crusty sill to listen
knocks aside the spare
roll of toilet paper.

A wood thrush trilling
to the amphitheater of storm-trashed limbs.

Fingers tally song-beats on the chipped paint,
commit the pattern: soft round chirps
before the crush of chatter notes—

Knot of sounds like crumpled tissue
a thrush throat snaps
strange between the dulcet coos

Faith

Dan and I lounged under an olive tree and laughed
        as the blindfolded do-gooders tried to pour dried beans
into red plastic cups without spilling. "This is hard!"
        came the wail over tuneful pinging—
cold beans against the card table.

Dan and I lounged under an olive tree and sighed
        as the loud man rushed toward us with the promise
of sight—"Just believe!" And all our blind sorrows would wipe clean.
He had a briefcase stuffed with tiny Bibles. Nothing
        in braille or large print—

Dan and I lounged under an olive tree and remembered
        that first time two like us waited by the road
to call for a good man. Others tell that story
        for the sleeping vision that broke bud—
        the restored sense that always takes precedence.
We tell it because the man hushed the crowd
        and asked what was needed.

Inside Jokes

A long draped table hosts five blind guests,
two microphones, one moderator:
a last supper strewn with free pencils, insufficient paper,
and clear water glasses.

In reaching for the only microphone that still works
my partner threatens to send
his decorous goblet tinkling to the floor—its thousand shards

a dark promise for the paws of our assembled guide dogs.

A second swipe for the mic
brings the glass an inch from peril, so he hands it to me.

I place it out of reach before the empty chair at my right.
No one mentioned the glasses when we sat down. No one filled
the water jug. No one brought an extra microphone,

so we pass the good one back and forth, rustling
the heavy mic stand along the disposable tablecloth, clinking the cord

against the overturned water glasses, bracing ourselves for the feedback.

Glass of Milk

He slides the spoon of fresh peanut butter
into my mouth—warm half moon
settling on my tongue. Homogenous.
Hint of sea salt. Smile widens
at my nod, and he passes me a cup.
A long draught and I hand it back.
We could be guests at a medieval table—
defining convivial, our bowl and goblet
stamped with the house crest. Instead we stand
at the sink, sharing cold milk in sheer blue.

Natural Compliance

The ramp ends here.
    It's a nice ramp, wide and well made. Room for us
        to walk side-by-side.
    An even surface—with sturdy wooden rails.
I can trail my hand along each
squared top (no splinters!)
    while the draping fronds
    waxy, shushing
        sweep readily out of my way.
But well-spaced wooden boards abdicate
to spongy earth, unpredictable roots—pockets
of soft sand. No match for the white cane
    I'm carrying.
Feet half-forward on the edge
I have options.
    I can place my free hand on the rail
        or on the worn narrow padding
        of your wheelchair's armrest.
A choice exacerbated
by the green breath ahead.

Trading Threes

Step out onto the lawn at dusk, dog leash
loose like reins in your fingers.
Over the quiet jingle of collar,
cardinal voices cross the yard.
Crisp patterns of two notes clinking
from separate trees, the cardinals stretch
the *ee* to *oo*. A line with two
repeats. The near bird calls,
gets an answer some way down the street.
A second response further away,
then back to the first. Touch of
overlap—another grabs on to that next
line. Always in the same key. No body
speeds up, slows down, backs off. All
volumes shaded by geography.

Sap

Sing down your length along your roots
Running golden sticky sweet
You fly inside all green things
Scent of oakmoss suspended
Of aging sun and burnt red leaves
Congealing fragrant on fingertips
Tides rushing under rough curtain
My ear pressed quiet to the bark
No shining shell to catch the ocean

Antiphon for Emily

We so Comfortably name her Recluse—
Spinster, sister, and Violet shrinking
Treasure her ribbon-wrapped bundles and dusty
Verses—to all ends enthrone this Ideal:

To Fix a scrawling woman in her Place—
insensible to Circumstances, merry
hands wave away cackling Contraries—
stitch close the frigates, funerals, Nobodies.

For our goal is Not to sip
the Liquor never brewed—Nor to
Trace the lava Step out of the neighbor's lamplight
But to Tame—Alas!—These ragged edges—
to weave Coherence Unshakable.

Small Hours

She shifts in her rented sheets, clicks off the lamp:
So you can't see their faces at all?
What do they look like to you?

No, I see hair, bodies mostly. The way someone walks,
how she carries herself. But I can't tell who wears makeup.

She turns on her side: So you don't know who's pretty?
Because some of them look kinda rough.

I'm grateful for the dark, the sudden hum of the air conditioner.
I guess I can't tell, not in that sense:
I don't really think about it.

You don't think about what we look like?

Not really.

She smiles: That must be so nice.
You're not hung up on it.

It's not a choice.

From the Plinth

He had all of it named before
I got here. The lovely chorus of trees
held pins in their bark. Scrappy
labels everywhere—tiny ribbons
testing a perfect breeze.

When we laughing slid down
against damp grass
pins snarled in my hair.
He pulled them out, one by one,
untangled papers from my curls.
Grass. Auburn. Woman.
Wife.
He tried my names on his lips—
all songs.

Now I hop from foot to foot—
marble stings the muscles
under my toes. Epithets circle
the base. I have come to represent
anything but myself. I want
a hand's help
stepping down.

Song

My ship sways on laughing seas
        Gentle fingers trace my arm
Smile I sense across the table
        His hand ever seeking mine

I've laid my cheek against his chest
        the solid earth that bears my weight.
I've filled my cup at hazel rills
        twinkling behind wire frames

His arms translate a circling strength
        the aging beech tree understands—
With rising crown and reaching limbs
        she touches her beloved friend.

Deficiencies

Under the table my guide dog lies nose-to-nose
    with a red-gold retriever named Conrad
their bodies poised in fragile silence
    that spotlights the rhythm of swaying tails.

I reach down to find muzzles close—
    unflinching at my touch. Two dogs
absorbed in each other. I wrestle

the sudden urge to tumble
my untailed body from this chair

to lie down and measure my worth
against their intimacy. But hesitation

comforts me. Delay eases the truth:
I'm only one kind of companion.

When He Calls Me Your Wife

We occupy the lobby in too-small chairs, hands
joined across a rigid armrest. The nurse calls
routine assurances around the swinging door: the schedule is moving
quickly folks & would anyone like a juice?

I sweep my thumb across your knuckles, over and over,
keep my eyes closed against the overhead lights.
Focus on the cozy cramp of familiar fingers.

At last we are summoned beyond the endless shuffling
of patients, the swinging door.
You ready for examination, I with my notebook.

The doctor hears that we are English professors,
trades diagnoses with lines from Chaucer—
a verse of Tyndale's Bible bisects the breakthroughs
from California. He lingers over the citation:
I see your wife writing it down.

Kiwano

Automatic doors crunch along their metal
guide—parting to allow us under the rows

and rows of fluorescents. With rattle
and sturdy hum shopping carts
cross the pale green floor.

Sale flyers whisper promises.
Cinnamon brooms wrapped in cellophane
huddle together, bristles skyward.

We conquer the sugar-flour haze rising
warm from perfect rolls and cakes,
plant ourselves among the stacks

of glossy globes. Red, green, yellow,
some apples dipped in splendid monochrome,
others mottled with careless elegance.

He presses each fruit into my hand
before dropping it in the sheer fragile bag.
My examinations are quick—fingers tracing

predictable curves, dimples, blemishes.
all these apples cupped in cardboard.

The last fruit wakes me up: unreality
in my open palm. Too large for my hand it flaunts
a surface of spikes, no gloss. A difficult shape.

Blindness Locked Me Out

The speed reading class for seventh graders
    slumped over tight columns of text spread flat
    on tables in the library where in her half-glasses
the kind mistress of mundane rentals said:
    just do your best. i don't expect a miracle.

The Friday dance nights for five dollars
    where antsy teens shuffled in a circle & the boys
        used too much drugstore cologne & the girls
        flaunted noisy earrings & strappy shoes.
i took a place in the circle, left my white
    cane on the sidelines, tucked in my purse.

The teambuilding tasks at orientation
    teaching trust by tumbling back against a net
    of classmate arms outstretched to catch
us—but how should i fall? i don't judge distances
    & can't scale the high tower where others are
fighting their fears & learning to fail.

4PM

My dog and I, routinely vacant,
move down whitewashed steps
into the grass—*sotto voce* crunch
beneath summer sandals. Leaves
skittering across exhausted asphalt,
the wind makes them sound older
than they are today.
Slim leather leash in my fingers,
I pause. Sun spears break
against the house, the porch
half in ragged shadow—everything
a little slanted.

In the Half-Light of Rehearsals

The smell of old sheet music, rarely replaced
The cold church, aisles lined with echoes
Pews swathed in scratchy monochrome.
In the choir pit ringed with straight-backed chairs,
sentinel lamps lit thin pages—waterstained—
Crinkling at every touch.
Choral fragments clinging to worn
hymnals—the score almost invisible
under clumsy annotations.

Green time

Soft sun, wool coat, warm coffee, crisp wind.
Raucous laughs—two distinct
    greetings.
        Strangers in passing.
    Voices
        I don't know.
Golf cart loud music lawnmower
    spilling leaves.

Inside a swell of familiar sounds
we sit close
    on a wooden bench,
    damp
        with morning dew.
I lean into your orbit
    and inhale
        woodsy cologne
            hints
            of orchid and plum.
Through my shades,
    your blurry outline
        ripples as you toss
        your head.

A Phenomenology of Blindness

It's not like walking through life with your glasses off.
I mean, sometimes we wear glasses, but they're different
from yours. Thicker, broader, darker. And they don't
work the quotidian miracle of correctable vision.

It's not like getting your eyes dilated once a year, staggering
out to the car under those stiff black shades with the sharp edges,
tearing up beneath the merciless sun and wondering how you'll manage
the drive home. Someone texted you but you can't read your phone.

It's not like groping in the dark when you come home late
and you can't find your keys because you and your girlfriends
had too many pomegranate martinis. I know it was a birthday,
but if you could think clearly, you'd know where your keys are.

It's not like leaving the nail salon after a pedicure, shuffling forward
in disposable flip-flips, doing everything you can not to chip that
gorgeous raspberry shimmer polish. It's not like that at all.

It's not like feeling faint because you forgot to eat lunch—you were
working so hard you couldn't even stop for a granola bar, so you
cling to your colleague's arm as he guides you outside. It's nice
to have support, you think, nice to know he doesn't mind helping.

It's not convenient, popular, or cumbersome. It's not a filter
that you can slide over the world, not a stylish coat hanging
in your closet. I, too, am waiting for winter because I love
wearing my coats—peacoats, swing coats, blazers. I have
so many! It's just that blindness isn't one of them.

Cello

It captures the sound of the earth,
creaking with the burden of revolution,
and the roots of great trees reaching deep inside,
curling round the axis. It sounds the dappled,
the luminous golden-green of thick foliage, of sunlight
lapping against wide, aged trunks. It rises,
richly sonorous, and pulls at each filament
of the spirit with familiar notes—the soft timbre
slides like warm honey. Thick, supple,
sweet, an old voice lives in the wood and the strings,
a cantor of primal invocations.
Tracing the gnarled bark and the wandering roots
to set the world reeling for rebirth.

Emily K. Michael is a blind poet, musician, and writing instructor from Jacksonville, FL. Since 2016, she has worked as the associate poetry editor for *Wordgathering: A Journal of Disability Poetry and Literature*. Her poetry and essays have appeared in *Wordgathering, The Hop-per, Artemis Journal, The South Carolina Review, The Deaf Poets Society, Nine Mile Magazine, Bridge Eight, Narrative Inquiry in Bioethics, BREVITY's Nonfiction Blog, Barriers and Belonging,* and *AWP Writer's Notebook*. Her first chapbook manuscript *Natural Compliance* won Honorable Mention in *The Hopper*'s 2016 Prize for Young Poets.

Emily's work centers on ecology, disability, and music. She develops grammar workshops for multilingual learners and delivers poetry workshops for writers at all levels. She regularly reads at Jax By Jax, a yearly literary festival celebrating Jacksonville writers. Emily is passionate about grammar, singing, birding, and guide dogs. Find more of her work at http://emilykmichael.com.

www.ingramcontent.com/pod-product-compliance
Lightning Source LLC
LaVergne TN
LVHW041602070426
835507LV00011B/1264